Thriving In Every Season of Life With God

Donna Louis

Thriving In Every Season Of Life With God
Copyright © 2020 by Donna Louis

All rights reserved. Printed in the United States of America. No part of this book may be used or reproduced in any manner whatsoever without written permission except in the case of brief quotations em- bodied in critical articles or reviews.

For information contact :
Donna Louis
http://www.MiracleBook.net

Book and Cover design by Donna Louis
ISBN: 9780578784335

First Edition: October 2020

DEDICATION

TO MY DARLING HUSBAND PATRICK WHO HAS ALWAYS SUPPORTED ME, ADVISED ME TO KEEP MOVING FORWARD, AND KEEP WRITING AND UTILIZING THE GIFT THAT GOD HAS BLESSED ME WITH.

TO MY BEST FRIEND DAWN WHO IS THE EPITOME OF A PERSON WHO THRIVES IN EVERY SEASON. SHE HAS SHOWN TRUE FORTITUDE THROUGHOUT HER LIFE. I AM HUMBLED TO BE HER FRIEND.

ACKNOWLEDGEMENTS

TO GOD BE THE GLORY WHO IS MY MAINLINE. I AM ETERNALLY GRATEFUL FOR GOD GUIDING ME THROUGH THE PROCESS OF WRITING THIS BOOK.

I AM GRATEFUL TO ALL OF THE PEOPLE WHO'S LIVES I HAVE SPOKE ABOUT IN THIS BOOK AND THE COUNTLESS OTHERS I WAS UNABLE TO MENTION DUE TO TIME FOR PRESSING FORWARD AND SHOWING GREAT LEADERSHIP AND BEING A BEACON OF LIFE FOR THE WORLD TO SEE THAT IT IS POSSIBLE TO THRIVE IN LIFE IN ALL SEASONS.

TO DON, I CAN NEVER SAY THANK YOU ENOUGH FOR BEING WHO YOU ARE AND TAKING THE TIME TO ASSIST ME IN EVERYTHING I ASK OF YOU.

INTRODUCTION

All of us have a dream. We all see a vision of what we would like our future to look like. In the Book of Proverbs, it states, "As a man thinketh in his heart, so is he", therefore it is so crucial to win the battle over our minds. If you have a mind-set of defeat, you will never thrive. You must see yourself as prosperous and successful, not whipped, or over-matched. If you always have it in your mind that you can never be prosperous and good things never happen to me then you are going against the thriving life that God wants for you.

When you see others thriving, there are seven major things that you must do so you can have this same success in your life. First you believe that it will and can happen for you. Second, you need to see a vision of thriving. Third, you must have faith. Fourth, you must have hope that you will thrive. Fifth, your words must reflect your desire to thrive. Sixth, you must have gratitude to thrive. Finally, you must trust God that he will make you thrive.

First, when you believe something, you accept it as true. Remember "The Wizard of Oz" movie when the scarecrow told the good witch Glinda "why didn't you tell Dorothy before she always had the power to go back to Kansas?" Glinda said, "because she wouldn't have believed me. She had to learn it for herself". Believing in yourself is important but believing in God's word it is vital to you thriving.

Second, for those of us who are blessed with sight, it is a beautiful thing. For those who are not that should never stop you from thriving because God enhances your other senses like hearing to balance things out. Stevie Wonder, Ray Charles, Helen Keller, and Andrea Bocelli are some famous people who are blind but have thrived in life. The Bible says, "where there is no vision the people perish." It is critical that you see yourself thriving always in all situations. You can thrive in every season of your life with God. Just see a vision of it.

Third, you must always have faith. In the book of Hebrews it states, "But without faith it is impossible to please him: for he that cometh to God must believe that he is, and that he is a rewarder of them that diligently seek him."–Hebrews 11:6. If you are the person who must-see things before you will believe them like doubting Thomas in the bible you are hindering yourself from thriving.

The Fourth thing is hope. God expects us to be hopeful always. Hope is a healthy outlook on positive energy. "For I know the thoughts that I think toward you, says the Lord, thoughts of peace and not of evil, to give you a future and a hope."–Jeremiah 29:11.

The Fifth thing you must have to thrive is gratitude. "Sing to the Lord and give him grateful praise. Make music to our God on the harp."–Psalm 147:7. The key to continual elevation in life is gratitude!

The Sixth thing is the words you speak. Your words will either elevate you or destroy you. "A man's belly shall be satisfied with the fruit of his mouth; and with the increase of his lips shall he be filled."–Proverbs 18:20.

The Seventh thing that you must do to thrive is trust in God. "Trust in the Lord with all thine heart; and lean not unto thine own understanding. In all thy ways acknowledge him, and he shall direct thy paths."–Proverbs 3:5-6. "Commit thy way unto the Lord; trust also in him; and he shall bring it to pass."–Psalm 37:5

It is possible for you to thrive when everything looks desolate. You must trust God. Every day that God gives you the breath of life that means this is another opportunity to thrive. You must look at thriving in another dimension other than financial. You should want to thrive in your health, breaking bad habits, in your marriage, staying in peace, and a host of other things. As we go through the different seasons of life get a vision of you being prosperous, and being victorious, thriving with God.

Chapter One

Resolve To Always Thrive

We all go through seasons in our lives, some euphoric and others despondent, however we must remember that God is always with us. God himself said, "I will never leave thee or forsake thee." There are many Bible characters that had their highs and lows in life such as Moses, David, Job, Joseph, Gideon, Ruth, and a host of others that we will speak about. All of them at one point or another did not believe they could thrive, but with God's help they did. They all encountered dark moments in their lives, but they overcame.

It is important to note here that dark times are times of testing. We will all at one time or another be placed on the Potter's Wheel and being molded and going through the fire is unpleasant. You may think you are perfect and that you can pass any test until the pressure is on. There was only one person in life that was perfect, and that was Jesus. Even Jesus felt the pressure, but he never caved, he thrived. When Jesus was in the garden of Gethsemane praying before they crucified him, his sweat was like droplets of blood to the ground. God is with you during these testing periods and if you will just listen for his still small voice, he will direct you and place you in a position to thrive.

SURVIVING VS THRIVING

Do you see yourself as just surviving or thriving? If you do not know the difference that is the first problem. God created us to reign in life because we are his children. If you are just looking to get by daily, then you are not expecting God's best in your life. When someone is just making it week to week financially, they are surviving. God wants you to thrive where you have more than enough to be a blessing to others. Sure, all of us will have times in life when things come against us in our health or other aspects of our life but none of us want to be in constant pain and in ill health. When you are thriving, you are prosperous and successful. You want that for every area of your life and so does God. Sometimes you will be tested, but if you really want to thrive in life, you will if you put in the work. Sometimes in life when you are just surviving it could be the environment you were raised in or events that have happened in your life.

In the Bible there is a woman named Ruth who was the daughter-in-law of Naomi. Ruth and her sister and Naomi along with their three husbands left Judah and went to Moab to escape a famine. Naomi's husband Elimelech along with the two sons Mahlon and Chilion unfortunately died and left just the women. Naomi advised her daughters-in-law that she was going to Bethlehem and not to follow her. However, Ruth told her wherever you go I will go. Ruth had great faith. Her faith and belief in God that he would provide for Naomi and herself since they were just surviving was solid. They introduced Ruth to a man named Boaz, and she proved to be a woman of integrity with Boaz. Ruth showed incredible character in obscurity. Boaz was a single wealthy man and Ruth went to work for him in the fields. Boaz fell in love with Ruth and she went from a lowly field worker to being Boaz's wife. The book of Ruth shows the workings of divine providence. The book reveals the extent of God's grace. God fully accepted Ruth into His elect people and recognized her with a role in continuing the family line into which his appointed king, David, and later His Son, Jesus, would be born. After Boaz married Ruth, she became pregnant and had a son they named Obed. This man Obed became the father of Jesse. Now Jesse was the father of David, who was in the direct family line of Jesus Christ. Ruth went from just surviving to thriving.

Last year in 2019 there was an incredible remake of the movie Aladdin. Now I know most of you if not all of you know the story of Aladdin. He is a poor street kid who is always being mischievous just trying to survive with his monkey Abu. By chance he meets Princess Jasmine and sparks of interest and intrigue surround them. Desperate to see her again after taking her bracelet he sneaks into the palace and the two fall in love with each other even though they are from two different worlds. After a host of adventures take place because of Jasmine's father's grand vizier Jafar who turned out to be his arch enemy Aladdin marries Princess Jasmine and lives a life of thriving. Aladdin had faith even though it was the size of a mustard seed that eventually he would thrive in life, and so he did. You can have the same, but you must have faith that your harvest season is coming.

WHEN YOU HAVE FALLEN AND FEEL LIKE YOU CAN'T GET UP

These are the times when you feel like someone has punched you in the gut and you cannot move. These are also the times when you just want to go to bed and cradle up in a fetal position and cry for hours. As a human being you can do these things, but eventually you must rise again. If you are a mother and you have young children, you will have to rise quickly to care for them. If you have a job eventually, you must return to work. If you are a business owner, you must get back in the saddle or else you could suffer loses. You cannot allow your feelings to take over your life because feelings change from moment to moment. This is where faith must kick in and you realize that if this happened to me, then I must be strong enough to handle it or else God would not have allowed it to happen.

There are two groups of people that are remarkably familiar with falling and having to get back up again. Babies start walking on average when they are 12 months old. Some start as early as 9 months old and some start at 18 months. The one thing all babies have in common is that once they start walking, they fall multiple times until they can walk perfectly. The other category of people is hockey players. Every hockey game has at least one player that falls on the ice during a game whether it is their unbalance, or they were tripped. They do not stay on the ice and refuse to get back up. They pop up and continue to play the game. If you want to thrive in life, you must get back up when you fall and keep a thriving mentality.

LIFE'S SURPRISES

As much as we all want to live an exciting, exhilarating life, we also do not want to be caught off guard and surprised. Unfortunately, surprises can be good and bad. You have just won a big contract for your business; you are the winning bidder on the dream home you wanted; you have won the office contest for writing the best travel article and now you will travel to Hawaii; you have just been approved for the four-year college scholarship you wanted, the results from your MRI have come back and the doctor says you don't need knee replacement surgery. These are many positive results in life surprising you.

However, when you are in a tough season of life, you may be surprised when your employer says they need to downsize and they are letting you go, you go to the doctor and are told you have pre-cancerous cells in your body; you go grocery shopping and when you come out someone has stolen your car, your sibling calls to inform you that your mother has just passed away unexpectedly.

These are some of life's surprises that test your faith. What you must remember here in these situations or similar ones is that you have been caught off guard and surprised, but it does not surprise God. God is not surprised about where you are right now. If things are bad, it does not take him off guard. He is not shocked about what has happened to you. God knows every situation we come into better than we can ever understand it. God was not surprised when Peter cut off a man's ear. He was not surprised when Jonah was swallowed by a whale. When Moses murdered an Egyptian. He was not confused when Adam and Eve bit into the fruit. God knows exactly what has happened and is happening in your life. He has allowed certain things to happen so he can mold and shape you into the dynamic person he has designed you to be. He will still get you to where you are supposed to be, and if it were going to prevent you from thriving, he would never have allowed it to happen. These are the times that we must trust God and stand strong and remain in faith, knowing that our thriving is right around the corner if we have stick-to-itiveness.

PRAYER

Many people have this backwards. They pray when all else has failed. This is not the way it works. You must pray first. Jesus was constantly in prayer while he was here on earth. There are countless times that we see in the Bible, Jesus prayed. Jesus prayed before he raised Lazarus from the dead. Jesus prayed in the garden of Gethsemane. Jesus prayed when he was nailed to the cross. Jesus prayed at his baptism. Jesus prayed before he chose his twelve disciples. As we can see from these examples Jesus considered prayer vital.

When trouble comes the first thing we should do is pray. Sure, you can call your friends and talk about the trouble with them, but the more you talk about it, the more upset you will become. You need to trust that God already has your answer. You must remember that God must always be the mainline and not the sideline! God has answers to problems that you will have 10 years from now, and the best part of it is that you will triumph and thrive.

Your prayer life needs to be simple. But thou, when thou prayest, enter into thy closet, and when thou hast shut thy door, pray to thy Father which is in secret; and thy Father which seeth in secret shall reward thee openly. But when ye pray, use not vain repetitions, as the heathen do: for they think that they shall be heard for their much speaking. Be not ye, therefore, like unto them: for your Father knoweth what things ye have need of before ye ask him. After this manner, therefore, pray ye Our Father which art in heaven, Hallowed be thy name. Thy kingdom come, thy will be done in earth, as it is in heaven. Give us this day our daily bread. And forgive us our debts, as we forgive our debtors. And lead us not into temptation but deliver us from evil: For thine is the kingdom, and the power, and the glory, forever. Amen. –Matthew 6:6-13. This is a remarkably simple prayer that Jesus gave us to pray.

If you think prayer does not change things and can make you thrive, then you never understood The Thai Cave Rescue of the Wild Boars Soccer Team. The tribulation begun on June 23, 2018 when assistant coach Ekapol Chantawong took the players on a post-soccer practice expedition that was supposed to last a few hours but the nightmare ended when the boys and their coach were rescued 17 days later. The coach and the soccer players were exploring the caves when a sudden storm caused the passageways to flood, trapping them inside. There were so many dangers involved in trying to rescue them that unfortunately an experienced former Thai Navy Seal diver did not survive.

The boys ranged in age from 11-17 years old, and their coach was 25 years old. It took 9 days for the divers to locate the players and their coach and 8 days to rescue them. Once the divers had located the boys, they played chess games with them and had them write letters to their parents. Prayer was at the forefront of this gripping human drama that played out in front of the world. There were countless people that played a part in this unbelievable dramatic rescue. One of the British divers Connor Roe recalled how he and two other British divers Jason Mallison Joshua Bratchley told the soccer team that "you've got two options here it's dive out and this is how we're going to do it, or stay in here but it's very likely you're not going to survive." These young boys and their coach realized that survival was highly likely, but they had to make up their minds they would come through this.

Since their rescue, the boys and their coach have been thriving! They granted the coach and 3 of the soccer players citizenship in Thailand. The soccer team traveled to Los Angeles and appeared on "The Ellen DeGeneres Show." The coach and the players appeared on ITV news program "This Morning" in Great Britain and National Geographic has produced a documentary about The Thai Cave Rescue.

What are the odds of such a miraculous rescue with so many people involved in this rescue that only one life was lost? Lt. Col. Saman Gunan, the retired Thai Navy Seal diver who died during the rescue mission, will forever be remembered for giving his life to this mission.

The power of prayer from around the world had this mission come to such a blessed ending.

HUMILITY VS PRIDE

Besides for having a negative mentality especially when things are not going the way we would like them to, this is another reason people do not thrive. We all give ourselves much more credit than we should. We think we know exactly how our lives should progress and end up. We make our plans but do not realize that God's thoughts are higher than ours. He has placed a gift (or gifts) inside of us and knows exactly what our purpose in life is. We should be humble and not prideful because we are incapable of doing anything if it is not for the grace of God. We have all been blessed with talents and creativity, but the reason we have these things are because of God. If you can do something easier than someone else, you must thank God for that. The Book of Proverbs has a lot to say about being a prideful person. "Let another man praise thee, and not thine own mouth; a stranger, and not thine own lips."–Proverbs 27:2. "When pride cometh, then cometh shame: but with the lowly is wisdom."–Proverbs 11:2. "A man's pride shall bring him low: but honour shall uphold the humble in spirit."–Proverbs 29:23.

God is the one who gives you power to get wealth and thrive. We must give the credit to God. In the bible there was a man named Gideon whom God had advised that he would give him triumph over The Midianites. He was a fearful man who stated, "O my Lord, how can I save Israel? Indeed, my clan is the weakest in Manasseh, and I am the least in my father's house." - Judges 6:15. Gideon gathered an army of

32,000 men to fight The Midianites army of 135,000 men but because God refused to share his glory with any man, he cut Gideon's army down to 300 men who defeated The Midianites. Gideon nor any of his men could claim that it was because of their might and strength that they won that war.

Being a humble person does not mean that you cannot do great things, it just means that you are not an arrogant person who believes it is all about me. When we are humble, we may believe that we are lowly and can never thrive, but this is when God reminds us, "He hath put down the mighty from their seats, and exalted them of low degree."– Luke 1:52

The genuine test to seeing how much humility a person has is to give them power and authority. Moses had murdered a man when he was 40 years old and ran away and was living peacefully as a shepherd in the desert for 40 years. However, Moses was given eminent authority by God to lead the people of Israel to the promise land, but he never let that power make him proud. Moses was a humble man because he acknowledged and obeyed God in all his ways. Moses oversaw the ruin of Egypt, had a direct authority over the nation of Israel, he had a dominating influence over the armies, Moses was the arbitrator for the people, as well as a host of other duties but Moses believed God. Moses had a speech problem but as we see here again just as with Gideon God used average people for the greatness of his glory. God will always make you thrive if you believe it yourself and step up to the plate.

YOU CAN DO IT

God is no respecter of persons, so if others can thrive, so can you! Until you get this deep down into your soul, it will not happen. Stop coming up with all the excuses: I'm too young, I have passed my time; I am too old, no one in my family has ever had success and thrived, I don't have enough education to be successful; I have never been lucky. This is just a bunch of negativities and if you hold on to it what has happened in the past is what you will continue to get in the future.

One of the biggest destroyers in life is FEAR = False Evidence Appearing Real. We are amid what we can only call a global panic attack. The pandemic increases our level of fear, anxiety, hopelessness, and depression. Nevertheless, we will survive. In the meantime, the media continues to stoke the fires, causing many of us to overreact and to respond in inappropriate ways.

First, there were news reports of people panicking regarding toilet paper and buying up all they could find. Now the news reported an increase in buying chickens. A business owner said he had a tremendous increase in sales because people are pouring into his business buying chicks expecting to ensure that they will have eggs. He explained how chicks cannot even have eggs for six months. He also pleaded that if those who buy them find they cannot do all the required elements to care for them to please return them to his store and he will buy them back. Now the latest thing is that the FDA is requesting that the makers of hand sanitizers please add denatured alcohol to the products to discourage people, especially children, from drinking the liquid. Hand sanitizers are meant for external use, they are not for ingestion.

According to the National Poison Data System calls from the month of March related to hand sanitizer increased by 79% compared to March 2019. This is profoundly disturbing and at the highest level of FEAR!

If you believe you will achieve. Your dreams and desires to thrive must be bigger than your fears. The Bible tells us you can do all things through Christ which strengthens you. Think about when you have food cravings, you will go out of your way to purchase what you desire to eat. If you must drive to the other side of town 30 minutes away to get what you desire, you do it.

They say you must do a thing 30 consecutive days before it becomes a habit. If whatever season you are in, you say I am thriving, eventually it will happen. The Bible says, "and calleth those things which be not as though they were." As long as we are alive life is going to happen. There will be things that arise that catch us off guard. That is when we lean in and pray not panic! We must keep our Bible closer than our fear." You can do it. Now let us begin to delve into our seasons and ensure that we thrive in each one with God.

DONNA LOUIS

Chapter 2

Winter Season

The winter season of our lives brings about a lot of reflection about the old and the new. This season in life is just like the weather seasons, which run from December to March of the next year. We laugh and smile about all the good things that have happened. We feel somber regarding the events in life that did not go well with us. Finally, we anxiously anticipate the future and what it holds. All these thoughts are part of the normal process of life and are not disastrous within themselves if we have control over our minds. The way we get into trouble is when we think too much and for too long. Sometimes we have a habit of reflecting on life like we are at the movies. We sit down, get a bowl of popcorn, and pull up a chair like we are settling in for an epic adventure. These are also the times when we see I, I, I, instead of God & I. You do not want to spend too much time reflecting on the past because that is exactly what it is: the past. Every new day God gives us another set of grace for the next 24 hours. No matter what any of us do, we cannot reverse the past and bring time back. We must look towards the future.

Farmers use the winter season to repair equipment and review plans for the next planting season. We also do the same thing when we start to think about what the New Year will bring and what we want to accomplish. Whether it is planning to overcome an addiction, lose weight, go to church regularly, read our bible daily, treat our spouse and family members better, get a better-paying job, strengthen our business with a greater client base, go back to college, be a better parent, etc. etc. There are several steps we can take in the winter season to begin to thrive in life.

THE DELETE KEY

I am in the process right now of typing this manuscript in word on my computer and sometimes I realize that I have made a spelling mistake. I do not wait until I have gone through the entire manuscript to correct a misspelling, I just hit the delete key and change what is wrong. This is the same process we must use in life. When we are in the winter season and reflecting on unfortunate things, we must hit the delete key and erase them from our minds or we can never move forward. What is in the past is in your rear! Think about it. The rear-view mirror in your car is just that it points and faces what is behind you and is small. However, your front windshield is exceptionally large and allows you to see what is in front of you. You must learn to delete things and look towards the future. Now do not get me wrong, some things will be easier to delete than others. If by accident you broke an irreplaceable family heirloom sure it hurts but the death or loss of a loved one will be harder to delete. You never forget that person, you keep them in your heart, but you cannot be despondent and cry every day because you do not allow yourself to heal or allow that person's spirit to be at rest. If they were a God-fearing person at some point, you must rejoice that they are now with God. Almost everyone nowadays has a cell phone. Your cell phone will notify you when you need to adjust. If you have a tremendous amount of pictures or videos or apps in your phone when it becomes too much your phone will let you know that you are running out of storage space and some items need to be either moved or deleted.

If you earnestly seek God and ask him to help you delete some things out of your life so you can move forward and start to thrive, he will. He will speak to you in that small still voice and advise you of the changes you need to make. Now, because of the rushed pace of life nowadays and the fact that we feel we always need to have something going on and noise everywhere, God can scream at you and you will never hear him. Now when your entire life turns upside down and you do not know where to turn and finally you drop to your knees in prayer, that is when God says now, I finally have your attention. It is particularly important that you realize that God is an ever-changing God, and he knows what is best for you. The same way you would not want to wear the same clothes everyday day after day just like the children of Israel did when they were in the wilderness for forty years God is constantly changing and strengthening your life. Don't despise hitting the delete key because most of the time what you have to delete is what will bring you up to a higher level in life and start you on your journey to thriving.

THE ISSUE OF BLOOD AND FAITH

Do you remember back in the Introduction of this book I spoke about how you need to have several things to thrive? A few of them that I mentioned you will see in this next story. One of them is faith. The Bible states, "But without faith it is impossible to please him: for he that cometh to God must believe that he is, and that he is a rewarder of them that diligently seek him."–Hebrews 11:6. God does not always expect us to have large faith. Sometimes it is small faith, but we must have some faith. "And Jesus said unto them, Because of your unbelief: for verily I say unto you, If ye have faith as a grain of mustard seed, ye shall say unto this mountain, Remove hence to yonder place; and it shall remove; and nothing shall be impossible unto you."–Matthew 17:20. If you have never seen a mustard seed, they are the smallest of all seeds on planet earth. However, when planted, they grow and become the largest of all garden plants. Now you know how huge a mountain is and if having faith, the size of a mustard seed can overtake a mountain then you realize how powerful faith is.

There was a woman unnamed in the Bible that had been suffering for a very long time with a health issue and no matter what she did and the countless doctors she saw and medicine she took, she was unable to receive healing. "And a woman having an issue of blood twelve years, which had spent all her living upon physicians, neither could be healed of any, came behind him, and touched the border of his garment: and immediately her issue of blood stanched. And Jesus said, who touched me? When all denied, Peter and they that were with him said, Master, the multitude throng thee and press thee, and sayest thou, who touched me? And Jesus said, somebody hath touched me: for I perceive that virtue is gone out of me. And when the woman saw that she was not hid, she came trembling, and falling down before him, she declared unto him before all the people for what cause she had touched him, and how she was healed immediately. And he said unto her, Daughter, be of good comfort: thy faith hath made thee whole; go in peace."–Luke 8:43-48. What an amazing testimony! This woman used all three concepts I spoke about. First, she believed deep in her heart that as soon as she had contact with Jesus that it would heal her. Therefore, she joined the crowds of people that were flocking to Jesus and reached for her healing. Second, she had a clear vision in her mind that as soon as she could contact Jesus even if it were just touching the hem of his garment that she would be healed of her blood issue. Finally, her faith in Jesus' healing power was her driving force that if she could be able to touch him in any form or fashion she would be healed. Look at the tenacity that she had. After twelve years she could have been despondent, dejected, depressed and a host of other negative feelings and emotions that engulfed her. Her crowning achievement and her thriving was hearing Jesus say to her, "Daughter, be of good comfort: thy faith hath made thee whole; go in peace." Thriving in life is very possible but you must do your part. God has a part and we have a part. How badly do you want to thrive?

IT'S BONE CHILLING COLD BUT YOU CAN START A FIRE

There are parts of the world where it gets bone chilling cold. Now I know you are going to say what does she know she lives in Florida. I used to live in New York, so I do know cold maybe not like Minnesota or Alaska where is gets bone chilling cold, but I have lived where is gets cold with snow. When it is so cold that even an infrared sauna may not be able to heat you up. There are also times in life when anything that can go wrong will. These are the times when you start a fire.

Some of us have been fortunate to have been in the Boy Scouts and the Girl Scouts when we were younger. One thing they taught you is how to start a fire. There are three components to starting a campfire: The Tinder–The Kindling–The Fuel. Now for our purposes we will refer to the tinder which is wood and say it is the Bible. We will call the kindling prayer, and finally we will call the fuel praise and worship. We have the capability to start a fire anytime, every day, even several times for the day. We are encouraged to do this from the Book of Joshua. "This book of the law shall not depart out of thy mouth; but thou shalt meditate therein day and night, that thou mayest observe to do according to all that is written therein: for then thou shalt make thy way prosperous, and then thou shalt have good success."–Joshua 1:8. Merriam-Webster defines thriving as being successful or prosperous. Well, this is what the previous Bible verse just stated we would have if we meditate on the word of God day and night. So, what is step one in this process we need to take out our Bibles, dust them off or in today's world of technology grab your phone or tablet and read and meditate on God's word.

Step two is the kindling which is prayer. Some people believe that if they pray some long drawn out prayer that God will answer them faster and be impressed with their long eloquent prayer. There are also people who are prayer intercessors who pray for others who pray loudly and with physical movements and hand gestures that believe God will hear and answer their prayers faster. God does not work on our timetable or at warp speed especially if people are not genuine when they pray. The Bible states what will be the results of those types of prayer. "And when thou prayest, thou shalt not be as the hypocrites are for, they love to pray standing in the synagogues and in the corners of the streets, that they may be seen of men. Verily, I say unto you, they have their reward."–Matthew 6:5. God instructed us how to pray, "The Lord is my shepherd; I shall not want. He maketh me to lie down in green pastures: he leadeth me beside the still waters. He restoreth my soul: he leadeth me in the paths of righteousness for his name's sake. Yea, though I walk through the valley of the shadow of death, I will fear no evil: for thou art with me; thy rod and thy staff, they comfort me. Thou preparest a table before me in the presence of mine enemies: thou anointest my head with oil; my cup runneth over. Surely goodness and mercy shall follow me all the days of my life and I will dwell in the house of the Lord forever."–Psalm 23. This prayer clearly encompasses everything and states that we will be in green pastures. God will lead and guide us and keep us by still waters, not disturbing ones. God will restore our soul and even though we are going through winter seasons, he will protect us where we do not have to fear. He will have us seated as the honored guest at a table with our enemies, which means we will triumph, and mercy and goodness will be with us always. This is thriving.

The third and final step is the fuel which is praise and worship. The word praise is listed 183 times in the Bible, depending on which version of the Bible you use. Now the word worship is listed in the Bible 71 times again, depending on the type of Bible you use. It is pretty apparent that praise and worship are two things that God expects us to do always to honor him. The list is endless of worship artists that have created albums honoring praising and worshipping God with their talent.

When you praise God in the winter season, that makes the devil mad. You are going against the grain because the devil expects you to be distraught, despondent, wallowing in self-pity and a host of other destructive mannerisms. You must learn to call those things which be not as though they were. When you are praising and worshipping God during the health issue, the financial concerns, the fear, the anxiety, the hopelessness, the depression and many other winter season issues that try to destroy your spirit and destroy your dream of thriving that shows God that you trust him and believe for the best and he will send his angels to comfort you, lift the burdens, and turn your situation around and bring you into your thriving season. So how do you handle the bone chilling cold? You start a fire and keep it going every day!

IF AT FIRST YOU DON'T SUCCEED TRY TRY AGAIN

If anyone was ever in a winter season where no matter what he tried did not work, it was Thomas Alva Edison. Thomas Edison is noted as creating the first electric lightbulb. Edison started testing designs back in 1878 with his team of researchers and finally filed for a U S patent in 1879. It is said that Edison tested over 3,000 designs for bulbs between 1878 and 1880. Thomas Edison founded the Edison Electric Light Company in 1878 in New York. Thomas Edison was once asked about his failures and he stated, "I have not failed. I've just found 10,000 ways that won't work."

Another person who spent some time in the winter season before they started thriving is Henry Ford. Mr. Ford filed bankruptcy twice before he could become prominent in the automobile industry. Henry Ford had a dream and a vision to invent a vehicle and believing that he was successful in 1986 quit his job and started the Detroit Automobile Company. Unfortunately, he was not savvy enough to handle his finances and was unable to repay his investors and had to file bankruptcy. Undaunted by what happened several years later with his vision still in front of him and his faith he tried again but he didn't brand and market his vehicles properly and again could not repay his investors and had to file bankruptcy for a second time. Having these two negative marks against him did not stop him from looking to succeed and thrive, he buckled down and tried again believing that the third time would be a charm and it was. Finally, he named the company The Ford Motor Company and never looked back. You must persevere, pray, and praise God in the winter seasons and let God do the rest.

FROM THE PIT TO THE PALACE

One of the most well-known talked about stories in the Bible is the story of Joseph. Joseph lived through 13 years of winter seasons when things were not going well, but Joseph was still blessed. Joseph had a dream that one day he would rule over his family and brothers. He relayed that dream to his siblings who were angry upon hearing this since he was the youngest son and loved more by his father Jacob who had also given him a special coat made of many colors. His brothers jealously planned to destroy him.

The brothers threw him in a ditch and sold him to merchants. He was ultimately sold to a high-ranking Egyptian named Potiphar. However, Joseph had favor and eventually became the supervisor of Potiphar's household. Potiphar's wife had an eye for Joseph and tried to seduce him. Joseph turned down her advances and one day Potiphar's wife caught Joseph by the cloak and again made sexual advances. Joseph fled, leaving his cloak in her hand. In anger, she falsely accused Joseph of attempted rape, and Potiphar put him in prison.

Even in prison Joseph had favor and was put in charge of all the inmates. While Joseph was in jail, he interpreted the dreams of two of his fellow prisoners. Both interpretations proved to be true, and they later released one of the men from jail and restored him to his position as the king's cupbearer. The cupbearer forgot about speaking to Pharaoh about Joseph's gift for interpreting dreams as he had promised hoping to get Joseph released from prison. Two years later, the king himself had some troubling dreams, and the cupbearer remembered Joseph's gift of interpretation. The king summoned Joseph and relayed his dreams. Based on Pharaoh's dreams, Joseph predicted seven years of bountiful harvests followed by seven years of severe famine in Egypt and advised the king to store grain in preparation for the coming dearth. For his wisdom, they made Joseph a ruler in Egypt, second only to the king. Joseph oversaw storing up food during the years of plenty and selling it to Egyptians and foreigners during the years of famine. The time frame for all of this was 13 years from the time Joseph had his dream until he lived his dream.

Jacob sent his other sons to Egypt to buy grain for them to eat so they would not perish and ultimately the brothers went and when Joseph saw them he denied them the grain until they went home and came back with now the youngest brother Benjamin and their father Jacob. It was great jubilation when they all met, and Joseph forgave his brothers for their evil. Through, the entire 13 years of winter seasons, Joseph still believed in his destiny. He kept his dream in his mind. He kept the faith and continued to hope. He was grateful that he received favor and oversaw all the inmates in prison. He waited patiently on God's timing and trusted him. Your thriving is just around the corner. It is closer than you think. Now let us see what the spring season has to offer.

DONNA LOUIS

Chapter 3

Spring Season

Spring is a wonderful time to revive yourself and get a fresh point of view about your life. We have passed Groundhog Day and realize that a new birth is coming in the form of spring. This season begins in late March and continues until late June. Spring brings lots of sunshine, warmer temperatures, the blooming of flowers and plants, and the birth of baby animals. When we think of spring, our thoughts go to the opportunity to exercise outdoors, fly kites, start doing gardening and many other things.

For those in the farming industry spring is the time of year once the ground is thawed out from the winter cold the farmers start to plant their crops. As soon as they have planted the crops, the farmers will use fertilizers, herbicides, and pesticides to spray on the crops to keep away unwanted insects. Once the crops are ready to harvest, this is good news for the rest of us because then we will have fruits, vegetables, and other items to eat.

Even if you have had a brutal winter season spring brings feelings of joy and hope of what is coming. Spring also brings daylight savings time and Palm Sunday and Easter Sunday. The last two being two of the most important days in the lives of believers of Jesus. This season will remind you that Jesus died for you and rose on the third day, and that alone will help strengthen your belief that you can thrive in every season of life with God.

PLANT YOURSELF FIRMLY

Since spring is a season of planting, you must plant yourself firmly starting with your mind and thoughts that you can and will thrive. The Bible says, "Those that be planted in the house of the Lord shall flourish in the courts of our God."–Psalm 92:13. Since spring is a time of cleaning, you start by throwing out all the old. The same way you might go through your closet and give away old clothes or even new ones that you just purchased at the spur of the moment, but you have never worn. Ladies, I am sure you may have a closet full of shoes, not like Emelda Marcos but still more than enough. Probably ¼ of those shoes you have never even worn. It is time for spring cleaning. Gentlemen, you know you do not need all those tools you have. You have so many you can open your own Home Depot, Lowe's, or Harbor Freight. Every time you could not find what you needed, you just went shopping and got more. It is time for spring cleaning for you as well.

The same way we spring clean our homes, we also need to spring clean our minds. It is like eating, if you keep eating too much of the wrong things you will gain weight and if you dislike exercising, it will only take longer to lose the weight. Ladies, if every time you have a nasty breakup and you reach for a gallon of ice cream you are not planting yourself correctly. Men if every time you get passed up for a promotion at work and you drown your sorrows in a guy's night out in your man cave that is also not planting yourself correctly.

Planting started since the beginning of time with God. "And the Lord God planted a garden eastward in Eden; and there he put the man whom he had formed."–Genesis 2:8. Renewing your mind with the word of God is planting yourself firmly. The Bible says. "And be not conformed to this world: but be ye transformed by the renewing of your mind, that ye may prove what is that good, and acceptable, and perfect, will of God."–Romans 12:2. Read the word of God and pray to God. He is the only one that can make you thrive.

In the Bible there is the story of Daniel. King Belshazzar wanted to understand an interpretation that was written on the palace wall and so he called in wizards, magicians, and astrologers and stated whoever could interpret the writing would be dressed in a purple robe and be given a gold chain of honor and would be third in power of the kingdom. Unable to decipher what the writing meant, they called Daniel since they knew he could interpret writings to come before the king. Upon arrival, Daniel could interpret the writing. Daniel advised the king he was not acknowledging God and praying to other spirits and this displeased God and he should change his ways. The king refused and, in that night, he was killed. Darius the median took over the kingdom and promoted Daniel. Darius immediately had Daniel dressed in a purple robe and given a gold chain of honor. King Darius appointed 120 governors to oversee the kingdom and additionally he chose Daniel and two others to supervise those governors. The supervisors and governors plotted to disgrace Daniel. They spoke to King Darius and advised him to make a decree if anyone prayed to other Gods besides him over the next 30 days should be killed. The king agreed. The governors and supervisors spied on Daniel and saw him praying three times daily to God and told the king. The king was distraught at this news but ordered Daniel to be thrown into the lion's den. A stone was placed in front of the den and they locked Daniel in. God sent an angel to lock the jaws of the lions for the night. The king spent a sleepless night and refused to eat. At dawn King Darius rose and went to the lion's den. Upon seeing that Daniel was alive and well, the king made a decree that everyone should fear, and respect Daniel's God and the king promoted Daniel as he said.

What Daniel did by keeping his feet planted firmly in God proved to God that Daniel was ready to give his life if necessary because God is who allowed him to thrive. After this event, Daniel continued to thrive even more. The Bible states. "Blessed is the man that walketh not in the counsel of the ungodly, nor standeth in the way of sinners, nor sitteth in the seat of the scornful. But his delight is in the law of the Lord; and in his law doth he meditate day and night. And he shall be like a tree planted by the rivers of water, that bringeth forth his fruit in his season; his leaf also shall not wither; and whatsoever he doeth shall prosper."– Psalm 1:1-3. Trust God and keep the faith and stay planted firmly and God will make you thrive.

FERTILIZE AND FILTER YOUR GROWTH AND DEVELOPMENT

The same way that farmers need to fertilize and use pesticides to protect the crops they have planted is the same thing that you need to do to ensure your growth and development leading up to your bountiful harvest in thriving. There are many ways that you can grow and develop your relationship with God, but let's look at the basic ones that you should do not only in the spring season of life but every day to cultivate your thriving.

God created us and saved us through Jesus because he wants to be in a relationship with us and that is accomplished in communication via prayer. Prayer is just talking with God about everything, just like you would have a conversation with a friend. There are no secrets hidden from God because he knows everything so you can talk with him about everything. God showed us how to pray in Psalm 23 and yes, this is a wonderful starting point. Tell him your needs and desires and pray bold prayers but always remember to add gratitude for all that he has already done for you and praise him for answering your prayers. You should pray to God all throughout the day. God never grows tired of hearing from you. The Bible says, "Do all this in prayer, asking for God's help. Pray on every occasion, as the Spirit leads. For this reason, keep alert and never give up; pray always for all God's people."–Ephesians 6:18.

Daily make time and get into the habit of reading your Bible. In the book of Joshua in the Bible it says, "This book of the law shall not depart out of thy mouth; but thou shalt meditate therein day and night, that thou mayest observe to do according to all that is written therein:

for then thou shalt make thy way prosperous, and then thou shalt have good success."–Joshua 1:8. We should never be too busy to take the time to read our Bible daily. Whatever is most important to us is what we give our attention to. God always must be the mainline, not a sideline. The minute you wake up in the morning, you should reach for your Bible and read. If you want God to make time for you and make you thrive, you must make time for God.

Being around like-minded people and going to church is vital to being successful and prosperous. "Let us not give up the habit of meeting together, as some are doing. Instead, let us encourage one another all the more, since you see that the Day of the Lord is coming nearer."–Hebrews 10:25. The company you keep can predict your future. It is important that you surround yourself with people that you want to emulate. "He that walketh with wise men shall be wise: but a companion of fools shall be destroyed."–Proverbs 13:20. If you are striving to become more like Christ, then you need to be in a great church where the preacher is correctly teaching the word of God. Going to church will be very instrument in your spiritual growth and development which will enhance your thriving.

In the Bible there was a man named Elijah who was a prophet who shared God's messages and warnings and encouraged people to believe that the Lord is God. Elijah was an obedient follower of God's word. He had many excellent qualities, which is the reason he received God's provision. Elijah was a man that was always listening for God's voice and was constantly in prayer. God performed many miracles through Elijah. God informed Elijah to seek out a young man named Elisha and anoint him to be his successor. Elijah found Elisha and spoke to him about being his disciple. Elisha left his family and followed Elijah. He watched him work and saw the miracles God performed via Elijah. When it came time for Elijah to die Elisha asked Elijah for a double portion of his spirit which means he was requesting a double blessing so he could do even bigger and better works than what Elijah did. Elisha did indeed go on to perform twice as many miracles as Elijah did. Elisha thrived twice as much as Elijah because he fertilized and filtered so he could grow and develop into what he wanted to become. You must do the same thing and then there will be no limits to you thriving.

THE TWO MOST IMPORTANT DAYS IN THE SPRING SEASON

Palm Sunday and Easter Sunday have always been symbolic and important to every believer in God, Jesus, and the Holy Ghost. These days and the times leading up to them are times of prayer, reflection, and thanksgiving. If it were not for Jesus who was sinless going to the cross for all our sins, we could never thrive in life.

When Jesus came riding into Jerusalem on the donkey, he was setting the groundwork for his crucifixion on the cross. Jesus humbled himself by riding in on a donkey which is considered in Eastern tradition to be an animal of peace compared to a horse which is considered an animal of war. Entering Jerusalem in the manner that Jesus did symbolized him as a Prince of Peace and not war. Jesus knew that he was marching to his death and that must have made his entry bittersweet. His deep love for all of us and his desire to please his father,

God Almighty is what kept him moving forward. Jesus continued to move forward which is exactly what he told the 10 men who had leprosy that he met while traveling through a village once when they cried out and said "Jesus, Master have mercy on us." Jesus advised them to go show themselves to the priests and because they kept moving forward to go to the priests as Jesus commanded them, they were healed. Jesus now sits in heaven on the right hand of the father, thriving because he was obedient and kept moving forward. You must do the same no matter what distractions come your way.

Easter Sunday is a day of new life and rebirth. Jesus rose from the dead and conquered all of Satan's evil devices. Easter is celebrated by children with Easter egg hunts. Some say that in the Christian community of Mesopotamia they used to stain eggs as a memorial of the blood of Christ. The egg is an ancient symbol of new life and rebirth, just like Jesus.

In the Bible there was a woman named Rahab. She was a Canaanite, and a prostitute. After the death of Moses and Joshua took over after 40 years in the wilderness, Israel was ready to take the land of Canaan and the first city in its way was Jericho. Joshua sent two spies to survey the land, and they went into the house of Rahab. Being that she was a prostitute and there were constant men going in and out the spies and Rahab figured they would not be recognized. They were wrong, and the king of Jericho demanded that Rahab turn over the spies. Instead Rahab hid the two spies from Joshua's army in piles of flax on her roof, telling the king's men they had already fled. Rahab believed that Joshua's men would overtake Jericho, and so she made peace with God and asked the spies to save her life and her family's life. The spies agreed to protect Rahab and her family and gave her a cord to hang from her home. When they returned, they destroyed every part of the city, but they left Rahab and her family unharmed. Rahab married a man named Salmon. Rahab gave birth to a son named Boaz who had a son named Obed who had a son named Jesse who became the father of David who was in the direct family line of Jesus Christ. So, Rahab is in the lineage of Jesus Christ. What a comeback from being a prostitute. Rahab received a new life and rebirth once she hid the spies that is thriving on the highest level, being a part of the lineage of Jesus.

DONNA LOUIS

Summer

Chapter 4

Summer Season

Summer season starts at the end of June and ends around the middle of September. There are constantly things to do. For a lot of people summer is the best season. The weather is much warmer; it is a great atmosphere to indulge in lots of outdoor activities, and especially for kids there is no school. There are two 3-day weekends during the summer season 4th of July and Labor Day which allows families to take long driving excursions, spend time at the beach, have barbeques, pool parties and many other fun activities.

Since there is so much physical activity in the summer season, we also need to keep our mental activity as sharp as well. We must continue to nurture the seeds we have planted in the winter and spring seasons about thriving and elevate our game by asking for big things. God will meet you at the level you are asking. If you are asking for small dreams instead of big dreams, then you have little faith in what God can do for you. Remember, faith is all about believing in the unseen. If you can see it then it is not faith. Jesus said if you have faith you can move mountains. This is what a man named Jabez did in the Bible.

JABEZ PRAYER

We find the prayer of Jabez in the Bible in 1 Chronicles 4:9-10. When Jabez's mother was giving birth to him she had a tough time and suffered much pain. After the birth she named him Jabez, which means pain, trouble, and sorrow. Imagine if that was your name and every time someone called you, they were saying hello pain, trouble, and sorrow. How are you today? This is the label that was placed on Jabez. Despite this label that was placed on him, Jabez had strong faith and knew how to ask big.

The prayer of Jabez is as follows, "And Jabez called on the God of Israel, saying, Oh that thou wouldest bless me indeed, and enlarge my coast, and that thine hand might be with me, and that thou wouldest keep me from evil, that it may not grieve me! And God granted him that which he requested." Wow, this is tremendous. Even with his name, Jabez prayed a bold prayer to God and God responded and answered him. If you want to just keep surviving, keep praying these small prayers to God, can you just give me a fifty cents raise, can you just keep my business afloat, can you just provide me the money to pay my bills every month? If you want to thrive, you should pray prayers like God bless me financially exceedingly and abundantly that I have more than enough for my needs and I have left over to pay someone else's bills. If you are dealing with a health issue pray God you promised by your stripes I am healed, I know God is restoring health back to me. Remember God said, "Ask, and it shall be given you; seek, and ye shall find; knock, and it shall be opened unto you: For every one that asketh receiveth; and he that seeketh findeth; and to him that knocketh it shall be opened."–Matthew 7:7-8. So, what are you going to ask God for?

THIS INSECT KNOWS HOW TO THRIVE

Ants are incredibly smart creatures. Ants may appear to be one of the weakest creatures, but they have wisdom that many men do not have. We are amazed at ants due to their work ethic - and as they march on in their single line to and from a food source until they have gathered every bit of it and taken it to their home. Though ants are very weak, they use wisdom to persevere and protect themselves. Ants thrive because of their determination and never give up attitude. When it is summertime they work diligently to accumulate as much food as possible, and they eat that in the Fall and Spring seasons when they are underground. The thriving mentality of the ant is that he prepares when he can for a time when he will need what he has prepared. This makes the ant exceedingly wise. Do you have the wisdom of an ant or can they teach you something about thriving? God says they can. "The ants are a people not strong, yet they prepare their meat in the summer."–Proverbs 30:25.

The ants use the summer to prepare for the Winter and Spring seasons, but they thrive and flourish in the fall season when they are underground. As you can see the summer season is a highly active time for the ants and this is the way it should be with you as well. Remember what I said earlier: God has a part and you have a part. If you will be diligent and do your part by preparing in the other seasons, then you will thrive when God brings you into your harvest season. Keep believing, keep your vision in front of you, keep the faith, keep hope alive, keep being grateful, speak what you desire, and always trust God to make it happen in his perfect timing.

HOW BAD DO YOU WANT TO THRIVE?

I was watching a show on TV last night called Court Cam. It airs on A & E and looks at some wild, crazy, emotional events that happen in courtrooms around the country. This episode had to do with a man who became a career criminal. Just before the judge announced the verdict, she said to the man we used to go to school together. The criminal broke down in tears when he realized she was correct and who she was. He just kept saying over and over, "Oh my God". He was overwhelmed with emotion to see where his bad choices in life had taken him, but when he was in school, they voted him as most likely to succeed. The judge announced her verdict and said she wishes him well when he gets out of jail with turning his life around.

Have your choices in life helped to keep you from thriving? Well if they have do not feel bad, don't think it's too late to change things and start thriving. No matter what friends or family may tell you God has the final say and God is not surprised where you are in life now. God can still get you to where you are supposed to be and the purpose, he originally created you for when you were in your mother's womb. Let us look at a man who had a 38-year delay.

In Jerusalem there was a pool called Bethesda, where impotent people who had many sicknesses and diseases waited to be healed with the moving of the water. As the story states an angel would come down to the pool at a certain season and stirred up the water and whoever was the first person to step into the pool would be healed of their sickness. Now Jesus came to the pool and saw this man that was sick for 38 years and asked him, do you want to be healed? The man said, "Sir, I have no man, when the water is troubled, to put me into the pool: but while I am coming, another steppeth down before me." "Jesus saith unto him, Rise, take up thy bed, and walk."–John 5. Immediately the man was healed of his sickness.

This man was dealing with this sickness for 38 years. In the past 38 years, he could never get close enough to be the first one to get in the pool after the angel stirred up the waters. How is that possible? How badly did he want to be healed? How badly do you want to thrive? What lengths are you willing to go through to reach your harvest season? Are you going to put in the work and ask big, pray constantly, believe for your harvest? Are you going to do your part and show God you trust his timing and you are in for the long run? Until you show God that you are going to keep doing the right thing no matter how long it takes or how difficult the seasons are you will not thrive. When you are going through these tough seasons that is your testing seasons from God. It does not matter how late in life you start to thrive remember what was said to Job, "Though thy beginning was small, yet thy latter end should greatly increase." – Job 8:7. It is never too late that is why you don't ever give up or give in because when you think it is too late because the pressure is too great that is when your miracle, harvest, and thriving is just around the corner. It is closer than you think.

YOU CANNOT PRAY FOR PRIME RIB AND THEN SPEAK CHICKEN

In the introduction I spoke about seven things that are critical to you thriving. The sixth one that I spoke about is the words you speak. Believe it or not, you may think this one is a simple task, but it is not. Honestly, it may be the hardest one of the seven. Why do I say that? In the Book of James, it says, "But the tongue can no man tame; it is an unruly evil, full of deadly poison." – James 3:8. We as people just casually fling words out of our mouth not realizing the repercussions they bring. It is especially important that we take time to analyze the words we are about to say before we speak them because what we say shapes our future especially when we pray and ask God for things.

We cannot pray to God and ask to be healed of a sickness and then when you are not cured immediately you say well, I knew it would not happen for me. Do not pray God help me to lose weight and be healthy and then say I dislike to exercise, and you keep eating unhealthy foods and drinks. You should not pray to God this apartment is too small, I want a big house and then say I know no bank will ever approve me for a home loan. Do not ask God for a brand-new car and then say what is the use I am living paycheck to paycheck now, so how will I ever be able to afford a car payment. You should not ask God for a baby and then say if I have a baby it will keep me awake at night when he or she is crying and I won't be able to keep the lifestyle I have now because I will be changing diapers all the time, cleaning up messes in the home, etc.

It is critical that you do not mix your words. You cannot have positive words coming out of your mouth in prayer and then speak negative words because they will cancel out the positive and prevent you from thriving. This applies to all words you speak. You cannot say I will not get sick this winter season and then as soon as two people in your office at work get sick you say oh well my time is coming, I know I'm next to get it. If you say I am blessed and then you didn't receive the promotion at work and then you say good things never happen to me you have just cancelled any future blessing that God had stored up to come your way.

In the Book of Proverbs, it says, "Death and life are in the power of the tongue: and they that love it shall eat the fruit thereof."–Proverbs 18:21. They say it normally takes 30 days for you to make a habit of something however don't chastise yourself if this does not happen because the tongue is such a small member of the body but extremely unruly. Ask God to help you with this one because this will be a game changer to lead you to a life of thriving. Can you conquer this YES because the Bible says, "I can do all things through Christ which strengtheneth me" – Philippians 4:13.

SET YOUR FACE LIKE FLINT

When you decided to get your driver's license, when you went to college and got your bachelor's degree, when you purchased that big screen TV, when you decided to purchase those golf clubs so you could learn to play golf you made a decision and did it. You set your mind on what you wanted to accomplish and did not deviate from the decision. This is the way you must stay on course and refuse to take your foot off the gas pedal until you reach your harvest and thrive in life. Are you going to encounter twists and turns? Of course! There are no straight roads to success. Research what you want to accomplish in life and read the stories of all of the successful people who are in the same field and you will see they had their ups and downs as well but they kept moving forward. Believe in what your dreams are. Have faith that you will accomplish them. Trust that God will bring you through.

This is what three young men named Shadrach, Meshach, and Abednego did in the Bible. They believed in God and refused to pray to any golden images that King Nebuchadnezzar said everyone had to pray to. The king made a decree that whoever refused to bow down and pray to this golden image would be thrown into a fiery furnace and burned alive. These three young Jewish boys refused to obey the king's orders and were thrown into the fiery furnace. They stated to the king they meant no disrespect but would not obey his orders. Furthermore, they said, "If it be so, our God whom we serve is able to deliver us from the burning fiery furnace, and he will deliver us out of thine hand, O king. But if not, be it known unto thee, O king, that we will not serve thy gods, nor worship the golden image which thou hast set up. The king was enraged and threw them into the fiery furnace and demanded that the furnace be turned up seven times hotter. The furnace was so hot that the king's men that he commanded to place Shadrach, Meshach, and Abednego in the furnace were killed from the scorching hot flames.

Eager for the three young Jewish boys to burn to death the king arose astonished when he saw four men in the furnace. The king questioned his men and said, "did not we cast three men bound into the midst of the fire?" They answered and said unto the king, "True, O king." The king then spoke and said, "Lo, I see four men loose, walking in the midst of the fire, and they have no hurt; and the form of the fourth is like the Son of God." The king then commanded that Shadrach, Meshach, and Abednego be released from the fiery furnace. The king then said, "Therefore I make a decree, That every people, nation, and language, which speak anything amiss against the God of Shadrach, Meshach, and Abednego, shall be cut in pieces, and their houses shall be made a dunghill: because there is no other God that can deliver after this sort. Then the king promoted Shadrach, Meshach, and Abednego, in the province of Babylon."

What is it that these three young men did? They set their face like flint. What is flint? Flint is a sedimentary cryptocrystalline form of the mineral quartz, categorized as the variety of chert that occurs in chalk or marly limestone. Flint was widely used historically to make stone tools and start fires. It occurs chiefly as nodules and masses in sedimentary rocks, such as chalks and limestones. –www.Wikipedia.com. Flint is massive and hard, and these three young men decided to be like flint and refuse to give in to the king's demands. This is what you must do until you reach your harvest, where you will be thriving and not just surviving. If it was going to be an easy road to travel, then everybody would do it. Truer words were never spoken by the late Steve Jobs, "I am convinced that about half of what separates the successful entrepreneurs from the non-successful ones is pure perseverance....

Unless you have a lot of passion about this, you are not going to survive. You're going to give it up."

DONNA LOUIS

Chapter 5

Fall Season

Fall season starts in late September and concludes in early December. The Fall season also known as Autumn is when the leaves change colors and fall to the ground and you see some of the most vibrant colors ever. Fall offers numerous food and drink items to partake of. Fall season is also the time of year when farmers get to see the reward of the growing season. Adults and children look forward to two events that take place during the fall season, which is Thanksgiving and Halloween.

Fall is known as the harvest season. Harvest means obtaining an accumulated store or productive result, to gather in or reap, to win by achievement. –www.Merriam-Webster.com. There is a poem called A Visit from St. Nicholas by Clement Clarke Moore which paints a picture of children who were nestled all snug in their beds, while visions of sugarplums danced in their heads. A sugarplum is a small candy in the shape of a ball or disk. –www.Merriam-Webster.com. Children love treats, and so do adults. When you come into your harvest season, it is like all your dreams have come true. You feel accomplished and happy. You are flying high; you have persevered, and you are finally thriving. Let us look at some stories of people that have come into their harvest and are now thriving. They do not differ from you. Like the Bible says, "God is no respecter of persons. What he has done for others, he will do for you."

GOD DECIDES TO SHOW OFF

In the Bible there was a man called Job who was very wealthy. Job was a responsible, upright, and sinless man. Job was a man of substance as he had been blessed by God exceedingly and abundantly. Job was married and had ten children. Job had an abundant amount of sheep, camels, oxen, and servants. Everyday Job would offer burnt offerings to God for all his family in case any of them had sinned in any way against God. Job is depicted as a simple man and a humble man whose heart was fixed on God.

One day Satan approaches God and tries to convince him that Job will stop worshipping him if his cushy life is taken away from him. Satan is given permission by God to punish and tempt Job to convince God that Job will turn on him. Satan attacks immediately and Job receives word that all his children, servants, livestock have all been killed. Job goes into deep mourning but continues to bless God amid the disasters. Satan witnesses this and God smiles but allows Satan another try. Satan then afflicts Job with horrible skin sores all over his body and at this point Job's wife encourages him to curse God and to give up and die, but Job refuses. Job receives a visit from his three friends, Eliphaz, Bildad, and Zophar who try to comfort him. Job instead of cursing God curses the day he was born. Job pays no mind to what his friends say. Bildad says to Job, "Though thy beginning was small, yet thy latter end should greatly increase." Job shrugs off what he says, and then a fourth man named Elihu converses with Job about his suffering and dilemma. This conversation took place in Chapter 8 of the book of Job.

Job was desperate to have a conversation with God and clear the air, but he still fears God and wanted to avoid evil. Elihu tells Job that when you suffer physically, it provides you an opportunity to see God's love and forgiveness when you are healed and brought back into prosperity. God sitting in heaven finally has heard enough and speaks to Job. God advises Job that he knows nothing about creation and how much power he has and to not question him. Job recognizes God's power and attests to his human frailty. God is pleased with Job's response; however, he is displeased with Job's four friends. Job intercedes on their behalf and God forgives them.

God restored Job's wealth, however he blessed him with twice as much as before. Job had double the amount of property, livestock, new children, and his health returned, and he lived another 140 years. What Bildad said back in Chapter 8 finally came to pass in chapter 42. God showed off to Job, his friends, and Satan that you can thrive at any stage and season in life with him.

DUMB AND DUMBER

Born in a suburb of Toronto, Canada called Newmarket and raised as a Roman Catholic Jim Carrey's family struggled financially. At an early age, Carrey knew he was a master of impressions and wanted to be in show business. Jim has three other siblings and he and his brother John worked eight-hour shifts after school as janitors and security guards in the factory where their father worked. Refusing to give up and having that thriving mentality, ultimately Jim dropped out of school and started to perform in comedy clubs while working at the factory.

After working and perfecting his act, he finally became noticed by Rodney Dangerfield. Eventually Rodney Dangerfield brought Jim to Las Vegas to perform. However, Jim decided he wanted to perform in Hollywood instead, and so he moved and started performing his comedy act at The Comedy Store. Jim still undaunted that he had not reached the success he wanted he made an adventurous decision and in 1985 wrote a check to himself in the amount of $10 million dollars for acting services rendered and dated it ten years in the future and kept it in his wallet. In November 1995 his belief, faith, determination, and vision became a reality when he landed the role in the movie Dumb and Dumber and was paid $10 million dollars. Jim reached his first level of thriving and has continued to soar since then.

THE HOUSE ON MANGO STREET

Sandra Cisneros is a Chicana writer and is best known for her book The House on Mango Street, which sold over 2 Million copies and has been translated worldwide into numerous languages and taught in classrooms. She has also authored several other books which have been translated into over twenty languages, including Spanish, Galician, French, German, Dutch, Italian, Norwegian, Japanese, Chinese, Turkish, and, most recently, into Egyptian, Greek, Iranian, Thai, and Serbo-Croatian. She is the only daughter in a family of seven children. Sandra has been called possibly the most famous Chicana writer and has been recognized as the first female Mexican American writer to get published by an influential publishing firm.

Sandra has worked as a teacher, a counselor, and has taught creative writing. She has also worked as an arts administrator, and as a visiting writer at several universities. Sandra lived several years in San Antonio, Texas and was a Writer-in-Residence at Our Lady of the Lake University. She has since relocated to Mexico.

Sandra's style of writing has been influential in the Chicana and Feminist literary field. Sandra likes to shine a light on issues such as gender inequality and relegation of cultural minorities. Since Sandra was the only daughter, she felt detached since her brothers stayed to themselves and her father spoke about his children as six sons and one daughter instead of stating he had seven children. This was the fuel that drove Sandra to write to detract from loneliness and despondency.

Sandra has founded two foundation The Macondo Foundation, an association of socially engaged writers, and the Alfredo Cisneros Del Moral Foundation. Sandra has received numerous awards for her writing and work. They awarded her the MacArthur Foundation Fellowship back in 1995, and one of the biggest was The National Medal of Arts from Barack Obama back in 2016.

Cisneros is proof positive of moving from just surviving to thriving by utilizing the gift that God has given her and progressing from season to season to where she is now living the life of her dreams and thriving.

THE IRON MAN

Records come and go in the game of baseball however the record that The Iron Man made in baseball maybe one that is never broken. I am referring to none other than the great shortstop and third baseman Cal Ripken Jr. Cal a former player has amassed many accolades which is why when he retired in 2001 baseball was losing one of the best.

Cal grew up in baseball because his father Cal Ripken Sr. was a player and coach in the Baltimore Orioles and Cal Jr. traveled around the United States with him. Cal Jr. was drafted by the Baltimore Orioles back in 1981 and reached the major leagues in 1981 as a third baseman, but the following year, they shifted him to the shortstop position. Right away Cal Jr. won the AL Rookie of the Year Award that year. Ten years later in 1991 he was named an All-Star and won the Home Run Derby and was the recipient of his first All-Star Game MVP Award. He also received his second AL MVP Award, and his first Gold Glove Award.

They gave Cal the title "The Iron Man" when he exceeded Lou Gehrig's streak of 2,130 that had stood for 56 years. Many people thought that was a record that would stand forever. However, Cal Jr. was a faithful player, and he always showed up for the game and gave his best. He did not miss one game in 16 years of playing baseball! That is a total of 2,632 consecutive games. He had a game in 1983 where he had hurt his hand but stayed in the game and unbelievably had five hits in that game.

We spoke about this quality of having faith back in the introduction. When God sees us being faithful day in and day out, he rewards this, and this is how you level up from surviving to thriving. "But the Lord is faithful, who shall stablish you, and keep you from evil." - 2 Thessalonians 3:3. "For I know the thoughts that I think toward you, saith the Lord, thoughts of peace, and not of evil, to give you an expected end. Then shall ye call upon me, and ye shall go and pray unto me, and I will hearken unto you. And ye shall seek me, and find me, when ye shall search for me with all your heart." – Jeremiah 29:11-13. God created us to thrive so step up to the plate and swing the bat!

ONE OF THE ORIGINAL KINGS OF COMEDY

You can call him a comedian, author, talk show and radio show host, motivational speaker, Mr. Family Feud, but Steve Harvey has moved from rags to riches, from surviving to thriving. Steve was born in Welch, West Virginia and has worked many jobs. He has been employed as a boxer, an autoworker, an insurance salesman, a carpet cleaner, and a mailman. However, he always believed and wanted to be on TV.

Steve started performing standup comedy back in 1985 and while he struggled to become a success, he was homeless for three years where he lived and slept in his car. Finally, he caught a break and became the host of It's Showtime At The Apollo Theatre and later on starred on TV in The Steve Harvey Show, which aired from 1996 to 2002. Ultimately, he became a part of the tour for The Original Kings of Comedy. Steve broke into radio and had The Steve Harvey Morning Show. Steve has also performed in several movies and authored several books including "Jump, Take the Leap of Faith to Achieve Your Life of Abundance."

Steve is a Christian and does quite a lot of motivational speaking. He uses his platform of "The Family Feud Show" to encourage people to realize you were not meant to live a life of just surviving but that you need to discover your gift, trust God, step out in faith and take a leap of faith and jump. Steve tries to teach people to believe, to trust, to write your vision, to condition your mind, to not lose faith in the process, to look towards your future, not your past. Steve keeps telling people you must put in the work to thrive. Steve says what the Bible says that God is no respecter of persons what he has done for Steve and others he will do for you.

Has Steve's story been an inspiration for many? Yes, it has as is evidenced where back in 2015 a portion of E 112th Street in Cleveland Ohio where his family moved to after leaving Welch, West Virginia was renamed "Steve Harvey Way" in honor of his accomplishments. God can take you places you never thought you would ever go, strive to thrive!

THE PRINCE OF PEACE

Arriving into this world being born in the humblest of ways in a stable and placed in a manger but thriving to sit on the right hand of God almighty is The Prince of Peace Jesus. Our savior Jesus came to earth sinless but had to endure all types of immoral acts and transgressions so he could complete his assignment that his father God gave to him, which was to save all of us. Jesus came to become the complete and final sacrifice for our sins.

For the time that Jesus lived here on earth, which is said to be approximately 33 years, he had good days and bad days just like we do. On the days that he was able to just sit in the temples and teach people I am sure were euphoric days because he was spreading the good news and the words of his father. However, on the days when he was being taunted, those were bad days. Nevertheless, he knew his purpose, and he did not cave. Jesus came to Jordan and was baptized by John and then was led by the spirit to go up into the wilderness to fast. Jesus fasted for forty days and forty nights, and when he completed this time was ready to eat. This is when Satan showed up to tempt him. Satan tempted Jesus three times trying to destroy him when he was in his weakened state because of hunger, but Jesus stood his ground and prevailed. How was Jesus able to thrive? Jesus believed in his father, God. He trusted him and had faith that he would never leave him or forsake him. That is exactly what God did because when Satan had lost and left Jesus, angels came and ministered unto him.

Jesus performed many miracles while he was here on earth because he was willing to step out and do the will of his father and knew his father God would be with him every step of the way. God never said it was going to be easy because if it were everybody would be doing what it requires to thrive. Jesus had to suffer tremendously before they nailed him to the cross for our sins. They arrested Jesus, accused him of blasphemy, and put him on trial. Jesus endured harsh interrogation. He was beaten, spit on, and mocked. Jesus was severely whipped, and finally convicted, and had to carry his cross to his own crucifixion. His hands and feet were nailed to the cross, and he was left hanging for hours before he died. However, Jesus rose from the grave three days later and got the victory and defeated Satan. He now sits on the right side of the father God in heaven and his name is the most powerful name.

Is thriving in every season of life possible with God? Yes, it is. Try it for yourself and if you stick with it and believe, keep your vision in front of you, have faith in God, stay hopeful always (don't go by what you see because God is always working behind the scenes even when you see nothing changing), be grateful always and in all things, watch the words you speak, and trust God always and when the timing is right, you will have your own testimony of how you have been able to THRIVE!

About The Author

Raised in New York Donna has always had a penchant for writing. Constantly surrounded by pen and paper Donna studied writing courses at Queensboro Community College in New York. She attended The Institute of Children's Writers and Long Ridge Writers Group in Connecticut. She moved to Florida and because of her relationship with The Holy Spirit she wrote a book on miracles.

Donna's first book Miracles of Direction Miracles of Conquest Miracles of Provision Miracles of Purpose helped readers explore miracles both past and present. The book explores biblical miracles that took place while Jesus was here on earth. She then references with miracles that take place daily in the modern world. She separates these miracles into four categories and presents insightful examples of each type, taken directly from the Bible.

Donna's latest published book, Book of Proverbs, Wisdom vs. Wilderness' delves deeply into the timeless human quest for wisdom.

The Book of Proverbs provides intellectual depth, insights, and exceptional wisdom on how to live a meaningful, joyful, and tranquil life by honoring and respecting God as omnipotent.

The new release discusses all chapters in Proverbs 1-31 and brings insight, clarity, and basic meaning to several verses in each chapter. It clarifies why wisdom is not only essential, but mandatory in life, if one hopes to live a blessed life, versus living destitute, empty, or feeling lost or hopeless.

Donna was chosen as the winner in the Authors Show 2018 Top Female Author Awards in the Religion/Philosophy/Spiritual category. They chose Donna from an international field of contestants by a panel of judges. They also chose her as a winner in 50 Great Writers You Should Be Reading in 2015, 2016, 2017 and 2018.

Donna has been married to her husband of 36 years Patrick Louis and lives in Florida. She lives to accomplish the task that God created her for and daily to follow Proverbs 3:5-6. "Trust in the Lord with all thine heart; and lean not unto thine own understanding. In all thy ways acknowledge him, and he shall direct thy paths."

www.ingramcontent.com/pod-product-compliance
Lightning Source LLC
Chambersburg PA
CBHW071413290426
44108CB00014B/1808